FRANCIS FRITH'S

BOSCOMBE AND SOUTHBOURNE

PHOTOGRAPHIC MEMORIES

ROGER GUTTRIDGE is one of Dorset's best-known journalists and the author of a dozen books on Dorset and Hampshire. He worked as reporter, chief reporter and deputy news editor for the Bournemouth Evening Echo before becoming a freelance writer in 1990. He is married to Sylvie and has a son, Andy.

FRANCIS FRITH'S
PHOTOGRAPHIC MEMORIES

BOSCOMBE AND SOUTHBOURNE

PHOTOGRAPHIC MEMORIES

ROGER GUTTRIDGE

First published in the United Kingdom in 2005 by
The Francis Frith Collection®

Limited Hardback Edition ISBN 1-84589-024-8

Paperback Edition 2005 ISBN 1-85937-967-2

British Library Cataloguing in Publication Data

Boscombe and Southbourne - Photographic Memories
Roger Guttridge

The Francis Frith Collection
Frith's Barn, Teffont,
Salisbury, Wiltshire SP3 5QP
Tel: +44 (0) 1722 716 376
Email: info@francisfrith.co.uk
www.francisfrith.co.uk

Printed and bound in Great Britain

Front Cover: **BOSCOMBE**, *The Beach* 72703t
Frontispiece: **BOSCOMBE**, *The Pier* 49157

*The colour-tinting is for illustrative purposes only, and is not intended
to be historically accurate*

Aerial photographs reproduced under licence from
Simmons Aerofilms Limited.
Historical Ordnance Survey maps reproduced under licence from
Homecheck.co.uk
Every attempt has been made to contact copyright holders of
illustrative material. We will be happy to give full
acknowledgement in future editions for any items not credited. Any
information should be directed to The Francis Frith Collection.

AS WITH ANY HISTORICAL DATABASE THE FRITH ARCHIVE IS
CONSTANTLY BEING CORRECTED AND IMPROVED AND THE
PUBLISHERS WOULD WELCOME INFORMATION ON OMISSIONS OR
INACCURACIES

CONTENTS

FRANCIS FRITH
VICTORIAN PIONEER

FRANCIS FRITH, founder of the world-famous photographic archive, was a complex and multi-talented man. A devout Quaker and a highly successful Victorian businessman, he was philosophical by nature and pioneering in outlook.

By 1855 he had already established a wholesale grocery business in Liverpool, and sold it for the astonishing sum of £200,000, which is the equivalent today of over £15,000,000. Now a very rich man, he was able to indulge his passion for travel. As a child he had pored over travel books written by early explorers, and his fancy and imagination had been stirred by family holidays to the sublime mountain regions of Wales and Scotland. 'What lands of spirit-stirring and enriching scenes and places!' he had written. He was to return to these scenes of grandeur in later years to 'recapture the thousands of vivid and tender memories', but with a different purpose. Now in his thirties, and captivated by the new science of photography, Frith set out on a series of pioneering journeys up the Nile and

to the Near East that occupied him from 1856 until 1860.

INTRIGUE AND EXPLORATION

These far-flung journeys were packed with intrigue and adventure. In his life story, written when he was sixty-three, Frith tells of being held captive by bandits, and of fighting 'an awful midnight battle to the very point of surrender with a deadly pack of hungry, wild dogs'. Wearing flowing Arab costume, Frith arrived at Akaba by camel sixty years before Lawrence of Arabia, where he encountered 'desert princes and rival sheikhs, blazing with jewel-hilted swords'.

He was the first photographer to venture beyond the sixth cataract of the Nile. Africa was still the mysterious 'Dark Continent', and Stanley and Livingstone's historic meeting was a decade into the future. The conditions for picture taking confound belief. He laboured for hours in his wicker dark-room in the sweltering heat of the desert, while the volatile chemicals fizzed dangerously in their trays. Back in London he exhibited his photographs and was 'rapturously cheered' by members of the Royal Society. His reputation as a photographer was made overnight.

VENTURE OF A LIFE-TIME

Characteristically, Frith quickly spotted the opportunity to create a new business as a specialist publisher of photographs. He lived in an era of immense and sometimes violent change.

For the poor in the early part of Victoria's reign work was exhausting and the hours long, and people had precious little free time to enjoy themselves. Most had no transport other than a cart or gig at their disposal, and rarely travelled far beyond the boundaries of their own town or village. However, by the 1870s the railways had threaded their way across the country, and Bank Holidays and half-day Saturdays had been made obligatory by Act of Parliament. All of a sudden the working man and his family were able to enjoy days out and see a little more of the world.

With typical business acumen, Francis Frith foresaw that these new tourists would enjoy having souvenirs to commemorate their days out. In 1860 he married Mary Ann Rosling and set out on a new career: his aim was to photograph every city, town and village in Britain. For the next thirty years he travelled the country by train and by pony and trap, producing fine photographs of seaside resorts and beauty spots that were keenly bought by millions of Victorians. These prints were painstakingly pasted into family albums and pored over during the dark nights of winter, rekindling precious memories of summer excursions.

THE RISE OF FRITH & CO

Frith's studio was soon supplying retail shops all over the country. To meet the demand he gathered about him a small team of photographers, and published the work of independent artist-photographers of the calibre of Roger Fenton and Francis Bedford. In order to gain some understanding of the scale of Frith's business one only has to look at the catalogue issued by Frith & Co in 1886: it runs to some 670 pages, listing not only many thousands of views of the British Isles but also many photographs of most European countries, and China, Japan, the USA and Canada - note the sample page shown on page 9 from the hand-written Frith & Co ledgers recording the pictures. By 1890 Frith had created the greatest specialist photographic publishing company in the world, with over 2,000 sales outlets - more than the combined number that Boots and WH Smith have today! The picture on the next page shows the Frith & Co display board at Ingleton in the Yorkshire Dales (left of window). Beautifully constructed with a mahogany frame and gilt inserts, it could display up to a dozen local scenes.

POSTCARD BONANZA

The ever-popular holiday postcard we know today took many years to develop. In 1870 the Post Office issued the first plain cards, with a pre-printed stamp on one face. In 1894 they allowed other publishers' cards to be sent through the mail with an attached adhesive halfpenny stamp. Demand grew rapidly, and in 1895 a new size of postcard was permitted called the court card, but there was little room for illustration. In 1899, a year after Frith's death, a new card measuring 5.5 x 3.5 inches became the standard format, but it was not until 1902 that the divided back came into being, so that the address and message could be on one face and a full-size illustration on the other. Frith & Co were in the vanguard of postcard development: Frith's sons Eustace and Cyril continued their father's monumental task, expanding the number of views offered to the public and recording more and more places in Britain, as the coasts and countryside were opened up to mass travel.

Francis Frith had died in 1898 at his villa in Cannes, his great project still growing. The archive he created continued in business for another seventy years. By 1970 it contained over a third of a million pictures showing 7,000 British towns and villages.

FRANCIS FRITH'S LEGACY

Frith's legacy to us today is of immense significance and value, for the magnificent archive of evocative photographs he created provides a unique record of change in the cities, towns and villages throughout Britain over a century and more. Frith and his fellow studio photographers revisited locations many times down the years to update their views, compiling for us an enthralling and colourful pageant of British life and character.

We are fortunate that Frith was dedicated to recording the minutiae of everyday life, for it is this sheer wealth of visual data, the painstaking chronicle of changes in dress, transport, street layouts, buildings, housing, engineering and landscape that captivates us so much today. His remarkable images offer us a powerful link with the past and with the lives of our ancestors.

THE VALUE OF THE ARCHIVE TODAY

Computers have now made it possible for Frith's many thousands of images to be accessed almost instantly. Frith's images are increasingly used as visual resources, by social historians, by researchers into genealogy and ancestry, by architects and town planners, and by teachers involved in local history projects.

In addition, the archive offers every one of us an opportunity to examine the places where we and our families have lived and worked down the years. Highly successful in Frith's own era, the archive is now, a century and more on, entering a new phase of popularity. Historians consider the Francis Frith Collection to be of prime national importance. It is the only archive of its kind remaining in private ownership. Francis Frith's archive is now housed in an historic timber barn in the beautiful village of Teffont in Wiltshire. Its founder would not recognize the archive office as it is today. In place of the many thousands of dusty boxes containing glass plate negatives and an all-pervading odour of photographic chemicals, there are now ranks of computer screens. He would be amazed to watch his images travelling round the world at unimaginable speeds through internet lines.

The archive's future is both bright and exciting. Francis Frith, with his unshakeable belief in making photographs available to the greatest number of people, would undoubtedly approve of what is being done today with his lifetime's work. His photographs depicting our shared past are now bringing pleasure and enlightenment to millions around the world a century and more after his death.

BOSCOMBE AND SOUTHBOURNE
AN INTRODUCTION

MORE than 200 years ago, on 4 August 1795, a stranger set off from the historic harbour town of Christchurch and headed west. 'From Christchurch', recalled the 5th Duke of Rutland later, 'we proceeded on horseback towards Poole. After going about two miles on the high road, we turned off by the advice of a farmer, who told us we should find a much shorter way by going to the left which, however, would not do for a carriage. We accordingly followed his direction till we came to the top of a high cliff, where we could not find the least track of a road. We were however in some degree recompensed by a most delightful view of the sea. After enjoying this noble scene, we turned our horses' heads in order to discover some road, which we at last effected. We rode as we thought in the direction towards Poole, for on the barren uncultivated heath where we were, there was not a human being to direct us. We were not, however, mistaken as, after a most dreary ride, we found ourselves on the high road, from whence we looked down upon Poole and its environs.'

The area that the duke was describing was Bourne Heath - the area we now know as Boscombe and Bournemouth. Two centuries

BOSCOMBE, *The Pier 1931* 84887

ago, there was hardly a building to be found here, apart from the odd cottage or farmhouse and the ancient villages of Holdenhurst and Kinson, which are now on the outskirts of the borough. Fishermen, turf-cutters and smugglers were the only regular visitors to the 'barren, uncultivated heath'. What the duke was not to know when his description was published in 1805 was that he would be one of the last out-siders to see the undeveloped Bournemouth. Four years later the Tapps Arms pub was built in what is now central Bournemouth, and in 1810 Captain Lewis Tregonwell, known as the 'founder of Bournemouth', started building a holiday mansion for his wife and family and effectively launched Bournemouth as a seaside town.

Boscombe - often called 'Bascomb' in old documents, perhaps a tribute to the regional accent - had, meanwhile, acquired a single dwelling of its own. Boscombe Cottage, owned by Philip Norris in 1801, stood in 16 acres of grounds a little to the east of present-day Sea Road and was eventually to become the nu–cleus of the Boscombe Manor Estate. The house changed hands four times over the next 50 years,

changing its name successively to Boscombe Alcove, Boscombe Lodge and Boscombe Manor. The last of these owners was Sir Percy Shelley, son of the poet Percy Bysshe Shelley. He bought it in 1849 for his mother, Mary Wollstonecraft Shelley, the author of 'Frankenstein', but when she died in 1851, Sir Percy and his wife decided to make Boscombe their home. In the second half of the 19th century, Boscombe Manor became an important cultural centre which attracted a succession of rich and famous visitors. The house even had its own 300-seat theatre.

In 1860, by which time Bournemouth was rapidly growing from a village into the nation's leading health resort, there were still only a handful of buildings at Boscombe, including one pub, the Ragged Cat, which later became the Palmerston Arms. Boscombe's growth really began in 1868, when the politician and former Foreign Office diplomat Sir Henry Drummond Wolff built himself a seaside home called Boscombe Towers close to the site of the present Burlington Hotel. He called the spot Boscombe Spa because of the mineral spring water which rose at the mouth of the chine and was bot-tled and sold as a health-giving drink. A small

BOSCOMBE, *The Bathing Beach 1925* 78783

thatched summerhouse was built over the spring, and visitors were encouraged to 'take the waters'. Sir Henry, hoping to make Boscombe a rival watering place to Bournemouth, opened his Boscombe Spa Hotel (now the Chine Hotel) in 1874.

In the same year, the Morning Post newspaper reported the rapid progress at this 'new place of refuge for the tired Londoner'. 'Somewhat less than six years ago the new rapidly increasing collection of villas known as Boscombe was a barren sandbank, a pine wood and a picturesque ravine or chine, at one end of which was a brick-field and kiln,' noted the reporter. 'The brickfield is now a pleasant garden and the sandbank is covered with pretty houses.'

In the last quarter of the 19th century, Boscombe grew rapidly, increasing its population from less than 300 in 1871 to nearly 10,000 in 1901. It acquired several fashionable hotels, numerous guest houses, its own pier to rival the one at Bournemouth, a shopping arcade, churches, schools, a theatre, a reading room and, in 1885, its own railway station. It was also annexed by the Bournemouth Commissioners in 1876, despite vociferous opposition by Boscombe people. Much of the development took place some distance from the sea, on either side of the road between Bournemouth and Christchurch, still known as Christchurch Road. It was not until about 1890 that the developments around Christchurch Road and Boscombe Spa expanded into each other. Much of the development was down to Archibald Beckett, whose commercial projects included the Colonnade at the corner of Christchurch and Palmerston Roads and, opposite, the Royal Arcade, the Salisbury Hotel and the Grand Pavilion Theatre, all opened in the 1890s. This Gothic terrace survives as the most imposing feature of Boscombe's pedestrianised shopping area.

As Boscombe Spa was taking its first steps as an infant resort, a short distance to the east a Bournemouth doctor was working out his own plans to transform another largely undeveloped area that we now know as Southbourne. Between 1870 and 1875, Dr Thomas Compton bought three areas of land which included more than a mile of coastline and Cellars Farm, which had good agricultural ground. He called his new estate Southbourne-on-Sea, and embarked on an ambitious series of projects designed to attract both residents and visitors. From 1871, he offered for sale 'numerous eligible building sites, charmingly situate, commanding fine marine and land scenery and close to the proposed South Bourne Winter and Summer Gardens'. The take-up was slow to start with, but gradually houses began to appear, most notably Foxholes, built for Henry Reeve, distinguished editor of the Edinburgh Review and the Greville diaries, leader-writer for The Times and literary adviser to the publishers, Longmans. To improve access to the area, Compton's company arranged for the construction of Belle Vue Road and initiated the building of Tuckton Bridge, opened in 1883 across the River Stour to Christchurch. On the seafront, 24 Trouville-type 'bathing boxes' were provided in 1875 for the use of bathers, rented out for 6d, or 4s for 12 tickets.

The centrepiece of Compton's 'Winter and Summer Gardens' was a huge glass building, bought second-hand and transported from Andover at a cost of £1,200 and re-erected between the present Bolton Road and the Crossroads in Belle Vue Road. Set in three acres of cliff-top grounds and opened in 1874, the Winter Garden was heated in winter and stocked with flowers and ornamental trees. It proved a popular attraction, at least in its early years.

But the most ambitious plan was still to come. In 1882, the Southbourne-on-Sea Freehold Land Company Ltd was formed, with Dr Compton among its directors, to continue development of the estate. In 1883, more than 20 years before the relatively-advanced Bournemouth began its Undercliff Drive, the Southbourne company started work on a promenade. Protected by a sea wall rising eight feet above the beach and with foundations nine feet below it, the Undercliff Esplanade consisted of a curved carriageway 40ft wide with a pedestrian pathway 16ft wide on the seaward side. The facility, which took two years to complete and cost £15,000, extended a third of a mile along the front. The esplanade was opened amid much pomp and ceremony, including a regatta and music by two bands. Flags and tubs of shrubs decorated the entire length of the esplanade.

In 1887, a year before Lady Shelley symbolically drove in the first pile of Boscombe Pier, Southbourne began building an iron pier of its own, which extended 880ft off the shore. It opened in August 1888 and 1,200 people passed through the turnstiles on the first day. The steamer 'Lord Elgin' provided a daily service from Bournemouth Pier to Southbourne and back.

Despite the general success of the various enterprises, time and tide took their toll, especially the latter. The Winter Garden survived for 15 years before being sold in 1889, while much of the agricultural land at Cellars Farm was lost to the sea by erosion. The Trouville-type 'bathing boxes' also survived for 15 years, but in 1890 all 24 were swept out to sea during a September gale. The esplanade and pier survived this disaster, but on 28 December 1900 a storm of 'exceptional ferocity' breached the sea wall and caused severe damage to the two-year-old pier. Further storms in January accentuated the damage. Although the promenade was not considered to be beyond repair, the owning company lacked the funds to carry out the work, and when yet more damage was sustained in 1902, the Undercliff Esplanade was finally abandoned.

SOUTHBOURNE, *The Cliffs c1955* S153102

13

The pier, too, was left unrepaired and was eventually dismantled in 1907.

By this time, Dr Compton had long since left Southbourne and moved to Devon, although he did return to the area in 1920 and died at Parkstone, Poole in 1925, aged 87. Despite the setbacks and disasters which befell the founder of Southbourne and his companies, development of the area continued apace for much of the 20th century; Southbourne eventually joined up with neighbouring Pokesdown and Boscombe to contribute to a conurbation which stretches almost unbroken from the western side of Poole to the eastern side of Christchurch. Together with Pokesdown and Winton, Southbourne became part of the newly-formed County Borough of Bournemouth in 1901.

In the years since then, Southbourne - which once boasted one of Britain's biggest prehistoric trading settlements at Hengistbury Head - has made several excursions into national or international history. In 1906, 30 Russian exiles led by Count Vladimir Tchertkov set up a colony at Tuckton House in Saxonbury Road. From the nearby waterworks, they printed copies of Leo Tolstoy's revolutionary writings for distribution to Russians around the world, including their homeland. In 1910, as a crowd of several thousand looked on at Southbourne Aerodrome, the Rolls Royce founder, the Hon Charles Rolls, became the first person to die in a flying accident in Britain when his aircraft broke in midair during a display and crashed. In 1921, the unfortunate school cook Irene Wilkins was battered to death by a blunt instrument near Seafield Road after being lured from London by a bogus telegram sent in response to her Situations Wanted advertisement. Her death became famous as 'the telegram murder'. Gordon Selfridge, founder of Selfridge's store in London and tenant of Highcliffe Castle, bought 700 acres of Southbourne and Hengistbury Head in 1919 with the intention of building a dream castle there. But his £1 million plan got only as far as the drawing board, and the land was sold in 1930. For the last half-century, Southbourne has been home to one of Britain's best-selling novelists, Frederick E Smith, author of '633 Squadron' and numerous other books.

HOLDENHURST, *The Village c1965* H296015

BOSCOMBE PIER

BOSCOMBE, *The Pier 1903* 49157

The paddle-steamers approaching and moored at Boscombe Pier are reminders that most piers started their working lives as landing stages for sea-going vessels. The dinosaur-like object on the pier is the skeleton of the famous 'Boscombe whale', washed up on the beach in January 1897. The pilot whale - 70ft long and weighing 40 tons - caused great excitement for miles around. The eccentric Dr Spencer Simpson bought the carcass from the Crown for £27, then hired a Brighton company to carve out and clean the bones. The blubber was left to rot on the beach, spreading a 'vile aroma all through the town' until council workmen removed it as a health hazard four weeks later. The bones were re-assembled in 1898 and became a popular attraction.

◄ BOSCOMBE
The Pier 1931 84887

Lady Jane Shelley, daughter-in-law of the poet Percy Bysshe Shelley, symbolically drove the first pile to begin construction of Boscombe Pier on 17 October 1888. The Commissioners of the Shelley Estate had refused requests to fund the project, so Sir Henry Drummond Wolff and others took matters into their own hands and formed the Boscombe Pier Company. The pier was never a huge financial success and was sold to Bournemouth Corporation in 1907. The main change on the pier from 1903 to 1931 was the addition of a theatre or pavilion at the pier head. The 'modern miss' in the foreground (bottom left) has sensibly tucked her skirt into her knickers to paddle in the shallows. With no hat and a lightweight dress, the woman calling to another young paddler (right) is quite informally dressed by the standards of the time.

◄ **BOSCOMBE**
The Pier 1908 61191

Boscombe was already an established and flourishing annexe to the main resort of Bournemouth by 1908, its cliffs and seafront lined by hotels and guest houses, including the Chine Hotel on the left horizon and the long curved terrace nearer the shore. Both hotel and terrace survive. A sign on the beach-side building below advertises 'refreshments'. The fashionable strollers on the pier epitomise the elegance that the town fathers sought for their Victorian resort.

◄**BOSCOMBE**
The Seafront 1913
66135

The original Boscombe Pier was very much a local product, designed by Archibald Smith of Boscombe and built by E Howell of the Waterloo Foundry, Poole. A feature of the pier was the viewing kiosks evenly spaced along its length. The buildings at the pier entrance possessed a certain grandeur, while the promenade had already acquired its modern look.

▶ **BOSCOMBE**
*The Promenade
1922* 72701

Given that the First World War has dominated much of the intervening period, it is hardly surprising that there have been no noticeable structural changes to Boscombe Pier and promenade in nine years. Fashions have changed dramatically, however, although hats are still almost universally worn, even on the beach. In the foreground, a man struggles to carry a pram across the sand.

◀ **BOSCOMBE**
From the Pier 1906
55907

Fine, ornate railings grace the side of Boscombe Pier, while on the skyline the Chine Hotel dominates the array of rather grand hotels. The white shed-like object with wheels on the ramp is a bathing machine. The three dark shapes on the beach are hooded basket chairs, made from woven strips of wood or cane, which offered shelter from the elements.

▲ **BOSCOMBE,** *From the Pier 1906* 55908

Despite the early date, the amenities on offer on Boscombe beach are surprisingly modern. Seafront facilities include a refreshment stall, hooded basket chairs and Saunders' 'fishing boats for hire'. The Pier Hotel (top left) and the other villas have all been replaced today by modern apartments.

◄ **BOSCOMBE**
The Cliffs c1960
B151023

The modern incarnation of Boscombe Pier is seen in the middle distance, although more concrete housing has been added to its supports since the 1960s. Bournemouth Pier can be seen one-and-a-quarter miles beyond. The cliff tops are devoid of much of the landscaping which was to appear later.

BOSCOMBE
The Beach 1955 B151022

In 1940, both Boscombe and Bournemouth piers were deliberately breached by explosives to prevent enemy landings in the event of a German invasion. This inconvenienced local people, who still needed to use them as working piers. The head and neck of Boscombe Pier were repaired in concrete in 1957-58, just a few years after this picture was taken.

ORDNANCE SURVEY MAP OF BOSCOMBE AND SURROUNDING AREAS c1907

THE BEACH AND THE PROMENADE

BOSCOMBE, *From the Pier 1900* 45232

Turn-of-the-century Boscombe looks strikingly devoid of the trappings of tourism which were to follow later. The Chine Hotel already dominates the skyline, but there is no sign of the stone arches which were soon to appear on the corner, while it would be another 14 years before the Undercliff Drive reached this point. The single beachside building is offering refreshments. Could the row of slot machines on the front of the building be offering What the Butler Saw entertainment? Far left are bathing huts and a horse, possibly employed to tow them into place.

24

BOSCOMBE
From the Pier 1918
68076

The horrors of the First World War seem a world away from the idyllic scene on Boscombe beach, here pictured during the last year of hostilities. The old-fashioned basket chairs are giving way to the modern deckchair, but beach lovers are dressed from head to toe for their day at the seaside. Of the sweep of stone arches, only the one on the extreme left survives to this day.

BOSCOMBE, *The Pier Approach 1918* 68074

An early form of the zig-zag path at the Boscombe end of the East Cliff can just be seen and survives to this day, albeit with fencing on each side. Again, it is hard to relate the picturesque scene to a world war, although most of those strolling on the beach will have mourned loved ones killed in the trenches during the previous four years.

BOSCOMBE
The Pier Approach
1922 72702

The little kiosk, bottom left, is still in place four years after picture 68074, page 25, was taken, but now a car has appeared on the scene. The heavy Edwardian dress code is undergoing a radical transformation, with the younger generation sporting much lighter wear, making the older matrons look as though they are from an earlier age.

BOSCOMBE, *The Undercliff Drive c1950* B151005

Motor cars enjoy the freedom of the Boscombe Undercliff Drive, which reached Boscombe in 1914 and Sea Road, Southbourne, in 1950. The flagstaff on the right looks much sturdier than its 1922 predecessor. Under the arches, people rest their weary limbs on deckchairs.

BOSCOMBE
*The Promenade
c1955* B151015

A similar view to B151005 a few years later finds the summer illuminations in place on the promenade, while the advance of the motor car has prompted the erection of posts and a barrier to restrict access to the Undercliff Drive. A roundabout has also appeared, complete with modern street lights (bottom left). To the right, ponies give rides to the more adventurous.

BOSCOMBE, *The Promenade 1922* 72706

The success of the Undercliff Drive prompted Bournemouth Council to provide permanent wooden beach huts in 1909. They were built to a uniform size and design at various points between Alum Chine and Boscombe Chine. Unlike the beach huts of today, those pictured had no front wall or door, but 'furnishing and decoration afford fine scope for the display of the taste and individuality of the different tenants'. Toilets were also provided. On the left, a speeding sign restricts traffic to 8mph.

◄ **BOSCOMBE**
From Toft Steps 1922
72705

Toft Steps were built to provide a pedestrian route from the East Cliff to the beach midway between the piers. While the first beach huts were said to be 'of uniform design', the variety of rooftops here suggests that that policy was short-lived. Boscombe Pier can be seen in the distance, and Hengistbury Head on the horizon.

◀ **BOSCOMBE**
The View from the Zig-Zag Path 1922 72683

The photographer was standing on the East Cliff looking towards Bournemouth Pier, with Canford Cliffs and Purbeck in the distance. Bournemouth Corporation built the zig-zag path from the top of the East Cliff during the winter of 1907-08. The cost of the project was £300.

◀ **BOSCOMBE**
The Sands and the Undercliff Drive c1955
B151006

The Undercliff Drive will celebrate its 100th anniversary in 2007, having been officially opened on 6 November 1907. The road between Bournemouth and Boscombe piers transformed access to the beach, although the scheme was a conservative alternative to a more ambitious but controversial plan to build shops and an electric tramway on the front and villas on the cliffside.

AROUND BOSCOMBE

BOSCOMBE
From the West 1918 68075

Two ladies pose for the camera on the cliff path overlooking Boscombe Pier. To the left of the flagstaff is a little summerhouse built over the source of the stream in Boscombe Chine. The building with white paintwork on its veranda and gable window (top left) was the Pier Hotel, since demolished.

BOSCOMBE
*Honeycombe Chine
c1955* B151004

Honeycombe, just east of Boscombe Pier, is the most easterly of the chines which break the cliffs at various points between Sandbanks and Boscombe. The first Boscombe house was built near here by Philip Norris in 1801. Originally called 'Boscomb Cottage', it appears on the first OS map in 1811 as 'Boscomb Alcove', and later became part of the estate developed by Sir Percy Shelley, son of the poet Percy Bysshe Shelley.

BOSCOMBE, *The Chine Hotel 1892* 31377

The hotel opened in 1874 as the Boscombe Spa Hotel and offered 'suites of apartments', a coffee room commanding views of the Channel, the Isle of Wight and the Dorsetshire coast, a smoking room and 'good saddle horses and carriages with careful drivers'. It was built by the Boscombe Spa Hotel Company, which aimed to create a first-class hotel with pleasure grounds and a winter garden. It closed in 1880 to begin a five-year spell as a school before reopening as the Chine Hotel. The building was greatly extended a few years later.

▲ BOSCOMBE
Sea Road 1913 66132

Once known as Shore Lane, the road
down to Boscombe Pier has been
Sea Road for the best part of a century.
The large building on the right was the
Pier Hotel. There is still so little traffic
that a young girl is able to adjust her cart
or doll's pram in the middle of the road.
A little further up the hill is a tiny donkey
cart. To its right, a lady appears to be
sitting on the pavement, perhaps after
taking a tumble. Another person kneels
beside her while others look on. Even the
man with the bicycle (left) has stopped
to look.

▶ *detail from* 66132

BOSCOMBE
Sea Road c1960 B151033

The Pier Hotel and other buildings have changed little in the 50 years since 66132 was taken, but the street scene has been transformed to cater for the age of the motor car. Street lights, traffic islands and road markings give an impression of clutter. Most of the people seem to be walking away from the seafront, perhaps heading back to their hotels for an evening meal. At the top of the hill is an open-topped bus - something that can still be seen in the summer months today.

BOSCOMBE, *The Arcade 1892* 31380

Arcades were a very Victorian concept intended to provide an extra attraction for shoppers on rainy days. There were already arcades in central Bournemouth and Westbourne when HRH the Duke of Connaught opened the Royal Arcade on 19 December 1892, the year when this picture was taken. The developer, Archibald Beckett, also built a theatre, the Salisbury Hotel, and other shops. These grand buildings in Christchurch Road were later extended from the gable end (right) in the same style and survive virtually intact.

BOSCOMBE
*Christchurch Road
1892* 31381

Our photographer was standing opposite Boscombe Crescent when he took this picture. How amazing that the chemist's shop (far right) is still a chemist's 113 years later - now Lloyds Pharmacy! But the Victorian cycle shop next door, indicated by the penny-farthing sign, has become a record shop. Opposite, the house on the corner has been replaced by a later office building. The adjoining terrace survives, although part of its frontage has been replaced with something less fancy and two of the five pieces of ornamental stonework on the roof have disappeared. The ironmonger's is now an Indian takeaway and a hair salon.

ENTERTAINING THE VISITORS

BOSCOMBE
The Chine Hotel c1875 8091

The Boscombe Spa Hotel, as it was then called, was only a year old in 1875 and much smaller than the extended building seen in later pictures. Even more significant is the thatched summerhouse in the foreground, built by Sir Henry Drummond Wolff beside the stream whose restorative properties gave the area its earlier name of Boscombe Spa. The spa waters were Boscombe's original raison d'etre and attracted many visitors.

BOSCOMBE
Boscombe Chine Gardens 1903 49160

Other features of Sir Henry Drummond Wolff's development of Boscombe were a rustic bridge (top left) and pleasure gardens running down the chine. In the intervening century, the rustic bridge has been replaced by one of concrete and steel, the steps have become a sloping path and the pond has been filled in and planted.

BOSCOMBE, *Boscombe Chine Gardens 1906* 55912

In an age when popular pleasures were much simpler than today, children could happily amuse themselves for hours by sailing boats on the pond. Little else has changed in three years, although girls are now in the majority and the grass on the island has grown, as have the trees, to the extent that they now obscure the rustic bridge.

BOSCOMBE
Boscombe Chine Gardens 1931 84888

Twenty-five years have passed since the Edwardian pictures on page 37 were taken but toy boats are still popular among the next generation of children. Theboys are equipped with hooks to recapture their straying craft. One boy, wearing a cap, is reaching out to retrieve his. If he fails, perhaps the young ladies could help, as they obviously don't mind getting their feet wet.

BOSCOMBE
From the Pier 1903
49158

Like Bournemouth, Boscombe's greatest asset as a resort has always been its sandy beach and safe bathing waters. At the water's edge are more than 20 bathing machines. Resembling beach huts on wheels, they were essential equipment for the fashionable Victorian and Edwardian seaside resort, allowing people to take to the water while retaining their privacy.

BOSCOMBE, *The Bathing Beach 1925* 78783

The crowds are reminiscent of the scene on a summer's day today, but very few seem willing to dip more than their toes in the water. In the background, changing tents abound. Both they and the open-fronted beach huts to the left are of uniform design.

BOSCOMBE, *A Beach Kiosk 1913* 66134X

This rather quaint kiosk sells all that a visitor could possibly want on a day by the sea at Boscombe before the First World War - including buckets, spades and soft drinks, some of them apparently placed in a basin in the shade to keep them cool.

BOSCOMBE
Looking East 1913
66129

Boats for hire are
another essential for
any self-respecting
resort, although
supply seems to be
exceeding demand on
this occasion. Even the
boat-keeper appears
to be absent.

▶ **BOSCOMBE**
The Beach
1922 72703

Nine years after 66129, page 42, was taken, the boats are still there, but at least the boat-keeper has returned and rolled up his trousers in the hope that someone might want to hire one. Deckchairs have appeared on the promenade, while fishing nets have been hung on the railings to dry. A soldier leans against them. The boy in the foreground has a towel over his shoulder and appears to be carrying a golf club.

◀ **BOSCOMBE**
The Pier Approach
1931 84889

In a country with unpredictable weather, it is important to provide theatres and other indoor entertainment. A sign above the pier entrance advertises 'The Good Companions' twice daily, at 3 and 8pm, presumably at the Pier Theatre. The Overstrand Café, later to become a licensed bar and restaurant, offers refreshments. Rock and ices can be bought from the kiosk to the left of the pier.

▲ **BOSCOMBE,** *The Promenade c1960* B151031

The art deco style of the Overstrand bar and restaurant at the Pier Approach give it the look of a 1930s cinema. On the forecourt, display boards show the menu and other information.

◄ **BOSCOMBE**
An Ice Cream Seller 1922
72702V

A traditional, striped ice cream stall tempts customers on the promenade. The sign to the right, looking more like an archery target, is in fact an 8mph speed limit sign. The speed limit today is 20mph. At the water's edge, people appear to be digging for bait.

BOSCOMBE
The Pier 1931 84886

The lead puppet's abusive, club-wielding antics may be politically incorrect today but there is no more enduring form of beach entertainment than Punch and Judy. In the sea beyond, a few hardy youngsters paddle in the shallows, while in the foreground both women and children tend to favour the cloche style of hat. The woman directly in front of the show is wearing a rather formal outfit, which seems inappropriate for the weather.

46

BOSCOMBE
The Beach c1960
B151029

Punch and Judy have moved to the east side of the pier entrance, and people are beginning to gather for the next show. The tide is in, and the hordes on the beach look a little hemmed in between the water and the seawall. This was a clear day, as the Isle of Wight can be seen on the horizon as well as Hengistbury Head.

BOSCOMBE, *Pony Rides c1955* B151012

Pony rides are another great seaside tradition, and in the old days no-one rushed to pick up the droppings. The purpose of the ladder and platform in the tree is a mystery. Across the road, below the union flag, an old wagon carries a cargo of harnesses, shafts and riding tack, while a child clambers on to the back of a carthorse.

SOUTHBOURNE
The Cliffs and the Bandstand c1955
S153016

Music is another way to entertain the visitors, hence the number of bandstands which appeared in public gardens around Bournemouth and, in this case, on the cliffs at Southbourne. The building has now gone, but public toilets now stand a few yards to the right and a café a little beyond. On the cliff edge to the left is the East Cliff lift.

BOSCOMBE
On the Promenade c1960 B151028x

Bournemouth and Boscombe have spent a century trying to shed their bath chair image, but for older people, the chance to laze on the front and take the sea air remains one of the great attractions. These ladies are enjoying a good gossip as they set the world to rights. Note the stylish, striped sunhat sported by the woman nearest the camera.

► **BOSCOMBE**
The Tennis Courts 1903 49161

The tennis courts which Sir Henry Drummond Wolff provided at the top of Boscombe Chine Gardens have recently been reborn as a basketball court! To the left of the path, there is now a mini-golf course. The grand building in the background was the Linden Hall Hotel, demolished some years ago and replaced by blocks of flats.

▼ *detail of 49161*

◄ **BOSCOMBE**
The Bowling Green 1913 66137

Bowls was another recreational option for locals and visitors alike, although regulation whites were clearly not the order of the day at this early date. In the background a mother and two unfortunate children can be seen grappling with the boredom of watching Granddad at play.

◄ **SOUTHBOURNE**
*The Riverside Inn, Tuckton
c1965* S153126

The inn is now called simply
the Riverside, but the scene has
changed little in 40 years. The
steel pontoon in the foreground
survives, minus the two sheds. The
inn is much the same, albeit with
a remodelled frontage. Tuckton
was rural until relatively recently,
and is called Tuckford in some old
maps and documents. In 1881, Dr
Thomas Compton founded the
Tuckton Bridge Company and built
a wooden bridge across the Stour to
Christchurch. In 1904, Bournemouth
Council built a stronger structure so
that trams could cross it.

BOSCOMBE FROM THE AIR *c1950* AFA109581

SOUTHBOURNE-ON-SEA

SOUTHBOURNE, *The Beach 1908* 61202

Dr Thomas Compton, one of several physicians who promoted the healthy qualities of the Bournemouth area's pines, heathland and bracing sea air, bought 230 acres and a mile of sea frontage at Southbourne in 1870 for £3,000. He called it Southbourne-on-Sea. Southbourne had a pier before Boscombe. Built in 1887-88 at a cost of £4,000, it was badly damaged by gales on 28 December 1900 and sustained even more damage in a second storm six days later. A much-shortened structure survived until Bournemouth Corporation demolished it soon after this picture was taken.

▲ **SOUTHBOURNE**
The Sands 1918 68060

The ugly lumps of concrete and a stairway
to nowhere could be all that survived of
the Southbourne Esplanade after it was
destroyed by storms in the early 1900s, or
perhaps the remains of a block of flats,
abandoned in 1888 due to erosion. A
third-of-a-mile of seawall and undercliff
parade had been built by Dr Compton's
Southbourne Land Company and opened
in 1885 by the doctor himself and the local
MP Sir Horace Davey. A toll was charged
for its use - 1d for adults and a halfpenny
for children. The company had insufficient
funds to maintain its creation, and was
later wound up.

◄ *detail from* 68060

SOUTHBOURNE
The Beach c1955
S153065

The square structure on the left is clearly a wall and is probably a surviving section of the Southbourne Land Company's ill-fated development. The dark shapes at the sea edge could also be remnants of the lost esplanade. Further along the beach, a chalet-style cafe braves the elements, while in the far distance the Isle of Wight and the Needles can just be made out.

SOUTHBOURNE, *The Beach, Foxholes c1955* S153058

With its masts and untidy fencing, this scruffy part of Southbourne would not have won any awards for landscaping in 1955, but 80 years earlier it was part of Cellars Farm, which Dr Compton bought in 1875. The farm included some good agricultural land, plenty of gorse and sand, and, in the north-west corner, a small oak wood named Foxholes. Much of the land has since been eroded by the sea.

SOUTHBOURNE
The Cliffs 1918
68059

Thirty years earlier than S153058, and taken a little to the west, this photograph shows quite a scrubby and wild landscape, yet a handful of houses have been built quite close to the sea. Despite the ambitions of Dr Compton and others, there is little evidence of the elegant resort that they dreamt of.

SOUTHBOURNE, *The Cliffs c1955* S153102

A similar view to 68059 from c1955 confirms that the houses have survived. The reef-like rocks, partially submerged by the high tide, may be the remains of the ill-fated esplanade. Note the distant jetty, which also appears in the 1955 picture of the beach at Foxholes.

SOUTHBOURNE
The Sands 1922
72709

Southbourne's narrower beach, sprinkling of pebbles and relatively limited amenities make it marginally less appealing for many beach-lovers - although it has advantages if you wish to avoid the densest crowds at the height of summer. In this picture only the children are dressed for beach play, although some adults lift their trouser-legs and summer frocks to stroll at the water's edge.

SOUTHBOURNE, *The Ravine 1922* 72717

Most geological breaks in the cliffs on this part of the coast are called chines, but this one is known as the Ravine or Portman Ravine. The name Portman occurs in various parts of Bournemouth, as it was the maiden name of Henrietta, second wife of Captain Lewis Tregonwell, known as 'the founder of Bournemouth'.

SOUTHBOURNE
The Ravine 1922
72718

Slopes and steps still connect the Overcliff Drive with Southbourne beach opposite Ravine Road today. It can still be a wild and windy place on a dark and stormy winter night.

SOUTHBOURNE, *The Promenade c1955* S153112X

Business is booming at the café in the background, judging by the tray of teas being carried by the man in the centre. The coats worn by most of the promenade strollers suggest that this was not one of Southbourne's hottest summer days. Despite this, one intrepid holidaymaker licks an ice cream in a deckchair.

SOUTHBOURNE
*Fisherman's Walk
Sands 1918* 68061

Fisherman's Walk takes its name from the distant days when fishermen used to follow a track down to the beach below the cliffs, arriving at a spot where they could expect to catch the best mackerel. After landing their catches, they would retire to the nearby New Bell Inn, the only pub for miles around. The East Cliff lift opened near this spot in 1908.

SOUTHBOURNE
The Beach 1922
72712

The eye is drawn to the lady wearing a cloche hat, on the skyline (top left). Behind her is a large marquee. Following the line of the cliffs to the right, we can see what are probably large houses or hotels. The beach huts along the promenade vary greatly in both colour and design.

SOUTHBOURNE, *The Cliffs 1922* 72711

Much of Southbourne was still undeveloped in 1922, although footpaths invite walkers to enjoy the fine views, which in this case includes Boscombe and Bournemouth Piers and the Purbeck hills beyond.

SOUTHBOURNE, *The Cliff Railway c1955* S153115

Work on the electrically-powered East Cliff lift had begun by the autumn 1907. When Lady Meyrick officially opened the lift in 1908, her husband confided his hope that they would not have to use it!

AROUND SOUTHBOURNE

SOUTHBOURNE
Foxholes, the Main Block c1955 S153046

In 1872 Henry Reeves, leader-writer of The Times and editor of the Edinburgh Review, bought land at Foxholes to build himself a home. It was the first house in Southbourne. He did not move in until March 1876, but was very happy there, commuting to London only for essential business purposes. A few years after Reeves's death in 1895, Foxholes became a girls' school named St Cuthbert's. An extra wing was added - the difference in style was easily discernible. In 1937, the Galleon World Travel Association bought the school and turned into a hotel. It was sold again in 1983 and demolished.

SOUTHBOURNE
Foxholes,
The Entrance Hall
c1955 S153028

In Henry Reeves's time, this room was the drawing room. The bas-reliefs around the upper walls were replicas of the Elgin Marbles in the British Museum. When the building was demolished, several people were keen to buy them, but they proved impossible to remove undamaged.

SOUTHBOURNE, *Foxholes, The Billiard Room c1955* S153032

There is more than a hint of the building's school past in this picture. The somewhat shabby billiard room looks suspiciously like a girls' dormitory or perhaps a gym!

SOUTHBOURNE, *Fisherman's Walk 1908* 61204

Two young nannies or nursemaids and their charges are among those who have stopped to pose for the camera. By 1908, the wooded path once trod by mackerel fishermen on their way to the sea had become a popular walk for local and visitor alike.

SOUTHBOURNE
Fisherman's Walk 1913 66138

The walk from Southbourne Grove to Southbourne Overcliff Drive retains an air of serenity to this day, although houses have mushroomed on either side and traffic noise is ever-present. The sign spells 'Fishermen's Walk' in the plural but most modern references use 'Fisherman's'. The woman with the perambulator wears a straw hat bedecked with flowers whereas her companion is more soberly dressed and could be the nanny. The old lady to the left of the lamp post, wrapped cosily in a rug, seems happy to be out and about. Her hat, coat, gloves and dark glasses contrast with the summer attire of everyone else.

SOUTHBOURNE
Fisherman's Walk
1922 72715X

Three young ladies pose for what appears to be a 1920s fashion shot, perhaps for a local store. The one on the right has ribbons in her hair in a romantic 1920s style. The two front costumes are similar, except that the sash on one sits demurely on the waist, while the other is worn in a more racy, dropped-waist style. The woman on the seat sports a hat.

SOUTHBOURNE
Fisherman's Walk
1922 72714X

Another fashion shot, perhaps, although the models look rather unnatural. The woman on the left has a tassel dangling from her waist and a lacy top with a beautifully scalloped edge. Around her neck is a long string of beads. The woman on the right is wearing a jaunty hat and has what appears to be a fur stole on her shoulders. Her dress is tunic-style, with a high-waisted sash, over a skirt. The woman in the middle is more plainly dressed. To the right is a bandstand, looking the worse for wear.

SOUTHBOURNE
Fisherman's Walk
c1955 S153009

The same bandstand, looking in much better condition than it did in 1922, is standing today. The scene is as typically 1950s as the previous pictures were 1920s. The families are heading for the beach, cardigans over their arms in case the sea breeze is cool.

◄ **SOUTHBOURNE**
Taking a Rest 1922
72713x

A gentleman and two ladies rest on a park bench during a summer stroll. The man has a cigarette in his right hand, while the woman at the other end of the seat looks for something in her bag.

◄ **SOUTHBOURNE**
The Gardens
c1960 S153098

The gardens run alongside Fisherman's Walk, and the scene has changed very little in 45 years. While one family looks at the goldfish, others rest on the seats to the right. One person appears to be an invalid carriage.

◄ **SOUTHBOURNE**
Belle Vue Road c1955
S153061

The scene in Belle Vue Road has changed little in 50 years, although most or all the shops have changed hands. Voysey's baker's shop (left) is now a mortgage broker's, while the National Provincial Bank next door has become a take-away food shop. Opposite, at the corner of Seafield Road, was the estate agent Fox & Son's. It later became a complementary health centre, but is now an accountant's. The seat (far right) has long gone, as have the power-lines for the trolley buses, which were phased out in the 1960s.

▶ SOUTHBOURNE
St Catherine's Road c1955 S153063

Here we are looking along St Catherine's Road towards its junction with Overcliff Drive and Belle Vue Road. The single-storey building at the end survives virtually unchanged as public conveniences. The call box in front of it could be the Tardis, but is more probably an old police box. A public telephone box now stands in its place but the light-coloured call box, halfway down the street on the left, has gone. The large gabled building behind the public toilets is now a surfing centre, distinctively painted pale blue. The white-fronted shop (near left), which was an Eldridge Pope & Co off-licence, is now Edna's Tuck Inn Café. The tobacconist's shop behind the site of the former phone box is today used for commercial storage. The post box outside survives. The sign on the building (far right) says 'Carey and Clayton works entrance'. It is now a commercial garage and workshop.

◄ **SOUTHBOURNE**
St Catherine's Road
c1955 S153062

This is a similar view to
S153063 taken from a point
further along St Catherine's
Road. Today the lamppost
and wooden fence and
gate to the right have been
replaced by the front gardens
of a row of bungalows. One
of them is occupied by
the Wessex Healthy Living
Foundation, which provides
complementary therapies.
The building at the corner of
Sea Road (far left),
which was Brereton's Stores
(W & E Lee), has been
restructured and is now a
private house. The Cross
Roads Fruit Stores next door
is now a home improvement
shop, while Hewitt, builder
and decorator, has become
a washeteria.

SOUTHBOURNE
St Catherine's Road
c1955 S153101

The public conveniences are now on the extreme right as we look the other way down St Catherine's Road. G O Moore is now Bradley's Restaurant, while the shop to its right (with canopy) houses a hairdresser. Beyond that is an ice cream sign, now the Schooner, another restaurant. Opposite, the chemist is now a take-away food shop. Two of the premises between there and the toilets remain a newsagent's and an electrical appliance shop, as they were 50 years ago.

◄ HOLDENHURST
The Village Green c1945
H296007

While Bournemouth grew up in Victorian times, the village of Holdenhurst on its outskirts is an ancient farming settlement, mentioned in the Domesday survey of 1086 as 'Holeest'. The word comes from the old English 'holegn' or 'holly', while 'hyrst' means copse. The white stones around the village green and the stripes at the foot of the lamppost may have been visual aids during wartime blackouts. Holdenhurst remains an idyllic scene just a stone's throw from the busy A338 spur road, the green now protected by wooden posts and sporting three beech trees.

◄ **SOUTHBOURNE**
Church Road
1900 45066

If any of the houses in this picture survive, they are lost in the sea of 20th- and even 21st-century apartment blocks and houses which cluster around St Katherine's Church. It appears to have been taken from a point near the church looking east or south-east. The scene underlines the totality of the transformation of this area in 100 years.

◄ **HOLDENHURST**
The Village c1965 H296015

The lamppost and stones have disappeared since H296007 was taken, and a tree has had time to grow between the cottages on the right. But the houses at the far end of the green look almost the same. On the left is New House and on the right Old House, otherwise known as Magdalen Cottage. The Wimborne banker William Clapcott is thought to have built New House in the 18th century. Magdalen Cottage is probably 17th-century. Behind it (out of shot but just visible in H296007) is a low, thatched, half-timbered building, believed to be the oldest in Holdenhurst. It is referred to in an old deed as the Hospice of St Mary Magdalen, but locals call it the Leper Hospital.

HOLDENHURST
The Church of St John the Evangelist c1945
H296001

The original Saxon church dated from Saxon times, but by 1829 it was in such a state of disrepair that restoration was ruled out. Instead a new, larger church was built on land nearby, given by Sir George Ivison Tapps. The first foundation stone was laid on 18 July 1833 by the second Earl of Malmesbury, and the building was consecrated on 9 November 1834 by the Bishop of Winchester. The Rev F Hopkins, who was curate from 1847 to 1850 and vicar from 1877 to 1903, added a new chancel in 1873 at his own expense.

HURN
Hurn Court c1955 H543005

Across the River Stour from Holdenhurst is Hurn Court, rebuilt in Gothic style around a 16th-century core by the second Earl of Malmesbury, who succeeded his father in 1820 and renamed it Heron Court. The family reverted to the original name around 1900. It became a school in 1952 before being converted into apartments in the 1990s.

INDEX

NAMES OF SUBSCRIBERS

The following people have kindly supported this book by subscribing to copies before publication.

Robert and Glenda Abel, Southbourne, Bournemouth

The Anderson Family, Southbourne

In memory of Arthur and Ann Barnes of Boscombe

Brenda A Bonsor, Southbourne

Betty Brown, Boscombe

D M Byrne, Southbourne

Jenny Hawkes and Paul Canfield

Mr P and Mrs M Chandegra, San Diego

In memory of the Clifton Club, 1959 - 1963

Lt. Colonel Brian Concannon, M.B.E.

Miss Zaphia Conn, Southbourne

Harry and Audrey Cook, Southbourne

Mr and Mrs D C Cook

John Cresswell, Southbourne

The Curtis Family, Boscombe Manor

The Dear Family, Southbourne

The Doel Family, Southbourne

My loving husband, Douglas, from Nina

The Dowler Family, Boscombe East 2005

Patrick Duncan

Granville and Hilda Edwards - Good Times

Mr Paul and Mrs Anne Eyles, Boscombe

R.I.P. David Faris, Noddy Train, Chine Gardens

Mrs Susan Foley

Mr T W Hall and Mrs R B Hall, Bournemouth

John C Harding, Boscombe

The Hawaiian Hotel, Boscombe

Osborne D Jenkyn, Clifftops

John Bryan Owen-Jones, Sheila, Peter and Family

Mark Terrence Jones

Pushka, Happy Memories, Family Kelly

Joan and Charles Kirk

Jamie and David Luke, "The Twins", Pursers Q.E.2

The Family of Peter Mallinson, with love

The Copestake, Feltham and Martin
    Families

In memory of Julius Mindel, East Cliff

The Minns Family

The Nicholls Family, Southbourne

Brenda and Colin Nyland,
    Pied a Mer 2005

Jane Oakley, Ken Oakley

Peter, Happy Birthday, December 2005
    from Reina

Mr C W Bennett, Ms H L Phillips,
    Boscombe

Carol and Rick Pipe, Southbourne

John C Reeve, Southbourne

Mike Robins, Boscombe

The Scott Family, Southbourne

The Simonis Family, Hengistbury Head

Gordon and Pamela Sisley, Southbourne

Suzanne and Gerry Smith,
    Bournemouth

G P Soden, Lilliput

John Tarrant

The Teasdill Family, Southbourne

Iris and Trevor, Southbourne

Chris Wakefield, Boscombe

Mr and Mrs D Wanklin

To Gramps, Geoffrey Wilkes, Boscombe

Miss Irene Williams and Family,
    Boscombe

Silver Wedding, Jim and Elaine Williams

FRITH PRODUCTS & SERVICES

Francis Frith would doubtless be pleased to know that the pioneering publishing venture he started in 1860 still continues today. Over a hundred and forty years later, The Francis Frith Collection continues in the same innovative tradition and is now one of the foremost publishers of vintage photographs in the world. Some of the current activities include:

Interior Decoration

Today Frith's photographs can be seen framed and as giant wall murals in thousands of pubs, restaurants, hotels, banks, retail stores and other public buildings throughout the country. In every case they enhance the unique local atmosphere of the places they depict and provide reminders of gentler days in an increasingly busy and frenetic world.

Product Promotions

Frith products are used by many major companies to promote the sales of their own products or to reinforce their own history and heritage. Frith promotions have been used by Hovis bread, Courage beers, Scots Porage Oats, Colman's mustard, Cadbury's foods, Mellow Birds coffee, Dunhill pipe tobacco, Guinness, and Bulmer's Cider.

Genealogy and Family History

As the interest in family history and roots grows world-wide, more and more people are turning to Frith's photographs of Great Britain for images of the towns, villages and streets where their ancestors lived; and, of course, photographs of the churches and chapels where their ancestors were christened, married and buried are an essential part of every genealogy tree and family album.

Frith Products

All Frith photographs are available Framed or just as Mounted Prints and Posters (size 23 x 16 inches). These may be ordered from the address below. From time to time other products - Address Books, Calendars, Table Mats, etc - are available.

The Internet

Already one hundred thousand Frith photographs can be viewed and purchased on the internet through the Frith websites and a myriad of partner sites.

For more detailed information on Frith companies and products, look at these sites:

www.francisfrith.co.uk
www.francisfrith.com
(for North American visitors)

See the complete list of Frith Books at:

www.francisfrith.co.uk

This web site is regularly updated with the latest list of publications from The Francis Frith Collection. If you wish to buy books relating to another part of the country that your local bookshop does not stock, you may purchase on-line.

For further information, trade, or author enquiries please contact us at the address below:
The Francis Frith Collection, Frith's Barn, Teffont, Salisbury, Wiltshire, England SP3 5QP.
Tel: +44 (0)1722 716 376 Fax: +44 (0)1722 716 881 Email: sales@francisfrith.co.uk

See Frith products on the internet at www.francisfrith.co.uk

FREE PRINT OF YOUR CHOICE

Mounted Print
Overall size 14 x 11 inches (355 x 280mm)

Choose any Frith photograph in this book.
Simply complete the Voucher opposite and return it with your remittance for £2.25 (to cover postage and handling) and we will print the photograph of your choice in SEPIA (size 11 x 8 inches) and supply it in a cream mount with a burgundy rule line (overall size 14 x 11 inches). **Please note: photographs with a reference number starting with a "Z" are not Frith photographs and cannot be supplied under this offer.**
Offer valid for delivery to one UK address only.

PLUS: **Order additional Mounted Prints at HALF PRICE - £7.49 each** (normally £14.99)
If you would like to order more Frith prints from this book, possibly as gifts for friends and family, you can buy them at half price (with no additional postage and handling costs).

PLUS: **Have your Mounted Prints framed**
For an extra £14.95 per print you can have your mounted print(s) framed in an elegant polished wood and gilt moulding, overall size 16 x 13 inches (no additional postage and handling required).

IMPORTANT!

These special prices are only available if you use this form to order. You must use the ORIGINAL VOUCHER on this page (no copies permitted). We can only despatch to one UK address. This offer cannot be combined with any other offer.

Send completed Voucher form to:
The Francis Frith Collection, Frith's Barn, Teffont, Salisbury, Wiltshire SP3 5QP